The Lowell Mill Girls

by Alice K. Flanagan

Content Adviser: Martha Mayo, Director,
Center for Lowell History,
University of Massachusetts, Lowell

Reading Adviser: Rosemary G. Palmer, Ph.D.,
Department of Literacy, College of Education,
Boise State University

COMPASS POINT BOOKS
MINNEAPOLIS, MINNESOTA

Compass Point Books
151 Good Counsel Drive, P.O. Box 669
Mankato, MN 56002-0669

Visit Compass Point Books on the Internet at *www.compasspointbooks.com*
or e-mail your request to *custserv@compasspointbooks.com*

On the cover: Nineteenth-century engraving of mill girls operating looms

Photographs ©: The Granger Collection, New York, cover, 4, 6, 7, 10, 12, 13, 22, 26, 31; Prints
Old & Rare, back cover (far left); Library of Congress, back cover, 40; Time Life Pictures/
Mansell/Getty Images, 5; North Carolina Museum of Art/Corbis, 9; MPI/Getty Images, 11;
Lowell Historical Society, 16, 18, 20, 21, 24, 25, 27, 28, 29, 30, 32, 34, 38; Bettmann/Corbis,
17; North Wind Picture Archives, 23; Hulton Archive/Getty Images, 33, 39; Massachusetts State
Archives, 37; James Marshall/Corbis, 41.

Managing Editor: Catherine Neitge
Designer/Page Production: Bradfordesign, Inc./Bobbie Nuytten
Photo Researcher: Svetlana Zhurkin
Cartographer: XNR Productions, Inc.
Educational Consultant: Diane Smolinski
Library Consultant: Kathleen Baxter

Creative Director: Keith Griffin
Editorial Director: Carol Jones

Library of Congress Cataloging-in-Publication Data
Flanagan, Alice K.
 The Lowell mill girls / by Alice K. Flanagan.
   p. cm.—(We the people)
 Includes bibliographical references and index.
 ISBN-13: 978-0-7565-1262-0 (hardcover)   ISBN-10: 0-7565-1262-X (hardcover)
 ISBN-13: 978-0-7565-1731-1 (paperback)   ISBN-10: 0-7565-1731-1 (paperback)
 1. Women textile workers—Massachusetts—Lowell—History—Juvenile literature. I. Title.
II. We the people (Series) (Compass Point Books)
  HD6073.T42U535 2006
  331.3'877'009744409034—dc22   2005002461

TABLE OF CONTENTS

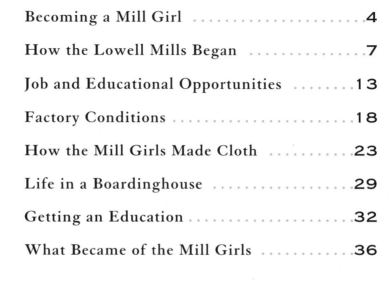

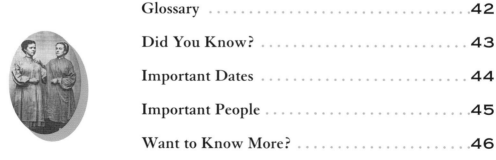

BECOMING A MILL GIRL

Ten-year-old Lucy Larcom jumped down from the large wagon that carried her family's belongings. It held everything her family owned. She and several of her siblings had arrived safely with their mother in the busy town of Lowell, Massachusetts, during the summer of 1835. Mrs. Larcom had been hired by a textile mill to run a boardinghouse where young women could live while they

An 1834 lithograph shows the factories of Lowell, Massachusetts, lining the water.

worked in the mills making cloth. At that time, Lowell cloth was sold and shipped to every part of the world.

As a boardinghouse keeper, Mrs. Larcom's job was to buy food, prepare meals, and take care of the women living there. She had been lucky to find work. After her husband died, she was left alone to care for the youngest of her eight children still living at home. The Lowell textile mills offered women like Mrs. Larcom a chance to provide for their families as well as educate their children.

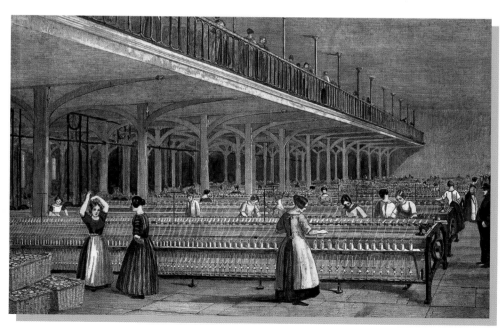

Women make cloth in an English textile factory.

Lucy Larcom wrote about her life as a mill girl.

A year after the Larcoms arrived in Lowell, Lucy went to work as a mill girl to help support the family. While working, Lucy also attended school part-time. After 10 years, she left the mills to teach and write. Years later she became a well-known author and poet. At a time when most women depended on men to take care of them, earning her own money was quite an accomplishment. It was American businessman Francis Cabot Lowell who made it possible for Lucy and other women to achieve this independence.

HOW THE LOWELL MILLS BEGAN

In 1813, Francis Cabot Lowell and other investors—including Patrick Tracy Jackson, Paul Moody, and Nathan Appleton—formed the Boston Manufacturing Company and opened a textile mill on the Charles River in Waltham, Massachusetts. It was the first mill in the United States to use machines to turn raw cotton into finished cloth.

Several New England textile mills spun raw cotton into yarn. However, none of them used machines to spin yarn and weave cloth in the same factory.

Nathan Appleton

7

England's water-powered looms were doing the work of many handlooms. Up to this time, British mills had successfully kept their machinery designs a secret. But in 1810, Lowell visited the mills in Lancashire, England, and then everything changed. When he returned to the United States in 1812, he asked mechanic Paul Moody to help design a water-powered loom like the ones he saw in England.

Then the investors of the textile mill in the tiny town of Waltham had to answer two important questions: What kind of cloth should they make? Where would they find enough workers? They decided to make cheap cotton cloth that they could sell to New England farmers, new settlers in the West, and people in other countries. Their workers would be inexperienced young women and men recruited from farms all over New England.

To interest young women and men in working at the textile mill, Lowell and the other investors built large boardinghouses where workers could eat and sleep under the care of a boardinghouse keeper, often an older woman. The mills offered wages that were better than women could earn as domestics or teachers, which were among the few jobs available to them at the time. And they paid their workers in cash at a time when most farm families had very little cash.

New England farms provided workers for the Lowell mills.

The only known portrait of Francis Cabot Lowell

Francis Lowell died in 1817 without knowing that the textile industry would bring the Industrial Revolution to the United States.

Four years after his death, Lowell's partners and other investors began looking for a new location to expand their textile mill and add calico printing. They found a site in East Chelmsford, Massachusetts, at the Pawtucket Falls on the Merrimack River.

In 1823, the Merrimack Manufacturing Company

began making and printing cotton calico cloth. It was cheap, costing "two and threepence" (37 ½ cents) a yard. The first calico print was deep blue with small white dots.

A label from the Merrimack Manufacturing Company

In 1826, a new town with 2,000 people was incorporated and named Lowell in memory of Francis Cabot Lowell. Twenty years later, the town of Lowell had a population of nearly 30,000. There were 10 large textile companies with 12,000 workers, mostly women. The "City of Spindles," as it was called, was by then the second largest city in Massachusetts.

An 1844 engraving of the Lowell mills on the banks of the Merrimack River

JOB AND EDUCATIONAL OPPORTUNITIES

News spread quickly about the opportunities at Lowell. By the mid-1840s, a great number of people from farming communities in Massachusetts, Vermont, New Hampshire, and Maine came to work in the town's textile mills.

An 1841 engraving of a cotton mill worker

The young New England women who came to Lowell usually worked there for four to five years. They came to earn money to help pay farm bills, send a brother to college, or care for sick parents. Others just wanted to save enough money to buy nice clothes for themselves or pay for a wedding. Men, a few with wives and children, arrived also, with their toolboxes in hand.

Everyone was interested in the educational opportunities that Lowell offered to its workers. Free schools were available for children nine months a year. Bookstores ran lending libraries with a membership fee of 25 cents a month. In 1844, the city public library opened with a membership fee of only 50 cents a year. There were evening schools for those who worked during the day. Lectures and public programs were offered almost every night of the week by a variety of groups in different locations, including Lowell City Hall.

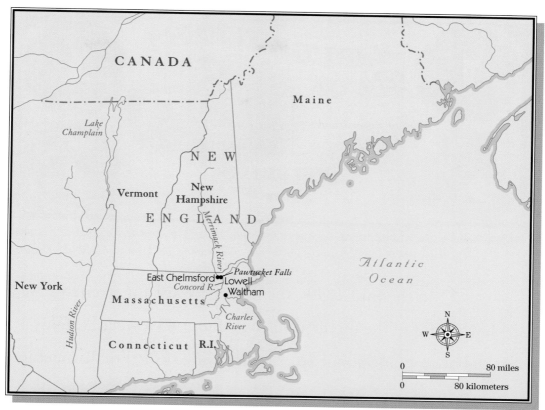

New England textile mills were built along rivers.

Of all the workers taking advantage of these opportunities, young women were the most interested in improving themselves. At the time, women had few formal educational opportunities open to them. In 1831, Lowell became the first town in the United States to establish a coeducational high school.

Until the 1870s, local banks printed their own money, backed by gold in their vaults.

In the mid-1840s, the average wage for women working in the textile mills was about $5 a week. (Male laborers made about $6 a week, while skilled male machinists were paid $9 a week.) Workers were paid in cash once a month. After paying for room and board, women usually spent a few dollars for clothes, treats, or classes and then put the rest into a savings account at the bank.

When the country girls with old-fashioned names such as Lovey and Florilla first arrived in Lowell, they must have been a curious sight. They came dressed in a variety of strange homemade fashions and had thick New

England accents. Some of them had their heads covered in heavy shawls pinned under their chins. Soon, these young women learned the "city way" of speaking and dressing. A few children under the age of 15 worked in the Lowell textile mills, like Lucy Larcom and Harriet Hanson, who came with their mothers. The largest group of workers was young women, and their average age was 22.

New England girls walk to work at a factory in a painting by Winslow Homer.

FACTORY CONDITIONS

The young women soon discovered that jobs in the textile mills were not difficult, but there were problems. They often stood for long periods of time and their feet hurt, although they found if they wore old shoes, it was more

An 1850s tintype of two young mill girls

comfortable. After about a year on the job, they discovered that their feet had grown and they would have to buy shoes a size or two larger.

In some rooms, the machinery was very noisy, so workers often stuffed cotton in their ears. It was so difficult to hear over the noise that workers talked with their hands. One girl recalled how it felt at the end of the first day in the weaving room:

"At last it was night. There was a dull pain in her head, and a sharp pain in her ankles; every bone was aching, and there was in her ears a strange noise, as of crickets, frogs and Jew's harps, all mingling together."

Many of the rooms were filled with dust and lint, and in the winter there were fumes from oil or gas lamps. In the summer when the weather was dry, the yarn broke easily. Mill managers closed the windows to help prevent this, but then the hot, stuffy air was difficult to breathe and some workers got sick. To care for their sick or hurt employees, the Lowell textile companies opened the first

Lowell Corporation Hospital

hospital for workers in the United States.

Each factory in Lowell had a tower that housed a bell, which rang to keep employees on time. One of the mill girls wrote about how the bells controlled their lives:

> *"Up before day, at the clang of the bell—and out of the mill by the clang of the bell—into the mill, and at work in obedience to that ding-dong of a bell—just as though we were so many living machines."*

During the summer months, the bells woke workers at 4:30 A.M. so they could be at work at 5 A.M. During the winter, work began at daylight. At 7 A.M., the breakfast bell

The Boott Mill in Lowell

rang and the girls hurried back to the boardinghouse for their first meal of the day. Then at 7:35 A.M., the bell called them back to the mills again. Work began 10 minutes later and continued until a noon bell rang for a 45-minute dinner break. At 12:45 P.M., the girls resumed work until closing time at 7 P.M. It would be many years before workers were able to successfully pressure the textile mill owners to

A Massachusetts mill girl stands beside a spinning frame in an 1845 engraving.

reduce the workday. And even this schedule is generous, compared to the early days when workers got only 30 minutes each for breakfast and dinner.

By the mid-1840s, most women in the mills worked between 65 and 72 hours a week. That meant they were putting in between 11 and 13 hours a day, six days a week. During the summer months, they might even work 14 hours a day. For all that, they were paid just under 5 cents an hour.

At first, there were four holidays a year when Lowell employees did not work: Fast Day, a day of fasting and prayer in the spring; the Fourth of July; Thanksgiving; and Christmas. All four were unpaid holidays.

HOW THE MILL GIRLS MADE CLOTH

Each step of making cotton cloth required knowledge of a different machine. The first step began in the picking house located close to the mill. There, male workers removed dirt and rocks from bales of raw cotton and separated it into loose fibers. Then, the raw cotton was taken into the mill.

In the mill, the cotton first went to the carding room, where workers placed the cleaned raw cotton into a "lapper." This machine combed the cotton, pulled out the knots, and wound it into thin, soft ropes called roving. The carding room was the dirtiest room in the mill. Dust and cotton fibers floated in the air.

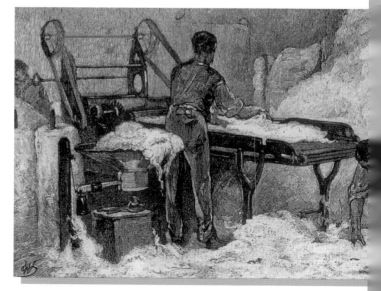

Workers remove dirt and rocks from cotton.

23

After the raw cotton was carded, it went to the spinning room, where long rows of spinning frames with spindles twisted it into yarn for weaving. The girls who worked in the spinning room were called spinners and doffers. Spinners watched the spindles wind the yarn onto small

A bobbin girl is hard at work in a painting by Winslow Homer.

spools called bobbins. If the yarn broke, the spinners mended it. They also kept the machines clean. As soon as the bobbins filled with yarn, doffers, or

Young doffers replaced bobbins on spinning machines.

bobbin girls or boys, replaced them with empty ones.

Doffers were the youngest workers, usually between 10 and 13 years old. It took them about 15 minutes to replace the bobbins, which had to be done once an hour. The rest of the time they could tell stories, sing songs, explore the other rooms in the mill, or go outside to play. To children, this type of work seemed more like fun than anything else. After a while, however, it became boring and the days seemed very long. Lucy Larcom wrote the following poem about her work as a bobbin girl at Lowell.

When I first learned to doff bobbins,

I just thought it play

but when you do the same thing twenty times—

a hundred times a day—

it is so dull!

The power looms in the weave room wove yarn into cloth. Many young women liked being weavers because they got paid by the piece and could earn more than other workers. Weaving took more skill than any other job.

It took skill to run a power loom that wove yarn into cloth.

An 1850s drawing of mill girls tending the looms

The last step in making cloth took place in the cloth room. Here the finished cloth was pressed, measured, and folded. Then it was separated into piles to be dyed, bleached, and sent out for sale. Workers in the cloth room received the lowest pay. However, the cloth room was clean and quiet. The girls could read while waiting for deliveries of finished cloth.

Reading books on factory time was against the rules. Nevertheless, girls hid books in apron pockets and wastebaskets. Often, they tore books apart and read them

The Song of the Spinners *appeared in a magazine in the 1840s.*

a page at a time. Sometimes they pasted poems to the windows or on their looms to memorize. Mill girls who were unable to read at work often recited poems aloud to one another or sang songs.

LIFE IN A BOARDINGHOUSE

Generally, between 15 and 30 young people from all over New England lived in each boardinghouse. The dining room was the first room nearest the front door. That made it possible for girls to eat their meals quickly and get back to work on time.

In the parlor of the boardinghouse, girls visited with their guests. Usually this room had a carpet and sometimes

Brick boardinghouses line a street in Lowell.

29

a piano. There were many bedrooms in each boarding-house, and most bedrooms had two beds. Two girls shared a bed in a small space crowded with books, boxes, trunks, and other personal items.

After supper, the girls spent their time sewing, reading, shopping, visiting, studying, going to church activities, or attending evening classes. They only had a couple hours of free time at night. At 10 P.M., the final bell rang, indicating there could be no more visitors in the boardinghouse.

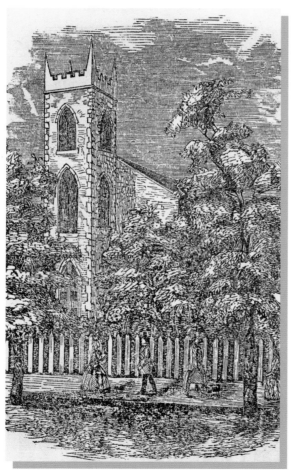

Mill girls attended church at St. Anne's.

An older woman or married couple managed each boardinghouse. They cooked, cleaned, cared for the boarders, and made sure the girls followed the company rules and regulations.

The rules were simple for workers living in a company boardinghouse:

Mill girls had to follow company rules.

- pay $5 a month for room and board;
- go to church regularly;
- be well-behaved;
- work in the mill for the length of their contract, often nine months, or give two weeks' notice if they wanted to leave.

GETTING AN EDUCATION

Education was very important for many of the mill girls. Whenever they were not working, they were involved in self-improvement activities. Reading was a big part of their efforts to improve themselves, and it eventually led to more serious studies. In the evenings, a few girls met in the boardinghouse parlor to study subjects that interested them. When several girls became interested in the same subject, they hired a teacher. It usually cost a dollar to attend 12 evening classes in subjects such as music, art, or French.

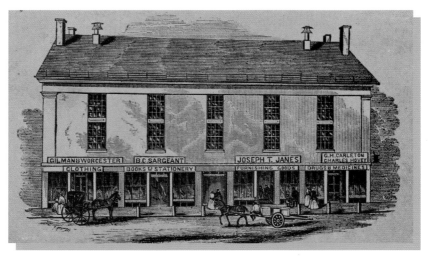

Mill girls would often attend lectures at the Lowell City Hall.

The girls also attended lectures, speeches, and special programs and concerts. They occasionally were able to leave the mills early to attend lectures by such gifted speakers as poet Ralph Waldo Emerson, writer Horace Greeley, and former U.S. President John Quincy Adams. Besides attending evening classes and lectures, the young women attended church. Ministers in several churches organized "improvement circles" where women brought their poems and other writings for discussion.

Horace Greeley

The Lowell Offering *was a popular magazine in the 1840s.*

Women had begun writing almost from the day the mills were established. By 1840, their writings were being published as a monthly magazine called the *Lowell Offering*. The small magazine, which was about 30 pages, cost 6 ¼ cents and was edited by two former textile workers, Harriet Jane Farley and Harriot C. Curtis. It was read by people all over New England and even outside the United States.

The *Lowell Offering*, which included poems and articles written by more than 60 women, became very popular. It covered topics such as women's rights, nature and religion, factory life, and local history of New England. One child remembered that her father "allowed her to read it on Sunday; and on that day it was placed on the table with the Bible."

The *Lowell Offering* was published until 1845, when Curtis left Lowell. In 1847, Farley started the *New England Offering*, which was also written by women. It was published until the 1850s.

WHAT BECAME OF THE MILL GIRLS

Over the years, the mill girls worked hard to improve factory and housing conditions. Sometimes they were successful. In October 1836, as many as 2,000 mill girls went on strike or "turned out" to protest a rent increase. They left their factory jobs to march through the streets and give speeches. They sang the following song:

> *Oh! isn't it a pity, such a pretty girl as I—*
> *Should be sent to the factory to pine away and die?*
> *Oh! I cannot be a slave, I will not be a slave*
> *For I'm so fond of liberty,*
> *That I cannot be a slave.*

The textile companies reversed the rent hike.

In 1844, the Lowell Female Labor Reform Association (LFLRA) was organized. Sarah G. Bagley, who worked as a mill girl, was its first president. The LFLRA was the first group of women to fight for a

10-hour workday. They sent petitions to the Massachusetts Legislature, which resulted in hearings to investigate working conditions. Their efforts proved somewhat successful when in 1847, the textile companies lengthened the time for breakfast and lunch from 30 minutes to 45 minutes.

In 1853, workers went on strike for a shorter workday, forcing the Lowell textile companies to shorten the workday to 11 hours. It wasn't until 1874, after a 30-year struggle, that the 10-hour workday became law.

Massachusetts became the first state to pass the

Sarah G. Bagley's name appears at the top of the second column on this 1846 petition.

or B. H. PENHALLOW'S
PRINTING ESTABLISHMENT,   } WYMAN'S EXCHANGE, CORNER OF
MERRIMACK AND CENTRAL STREETS, LOWELL.

1864.

TIME TABLE OF THE LOWELL MILLS,

Arranged to make the working time for ten years average 11 hours per day.

The STANDARD TIME will be marked at noon, by the BELL of the
MERRIMACK MANUFACTURING COMPANY.

During January and December.

COMMENCE WORK, at 7 A. M. STOP WORK, at 7 P. M., except on Saturday Evenings.
BREAKFAST at 6.30 A. M. DINNER, at 12.30 P. M. Commence Work, after dinner, 1.15 P. M.

From 1st of February to November 30th, inclusive.

COMMENCE WORK at 6.30 A. M. STOP WORK, at 6.30 P. M., except on Saturday Evenings.
BREAKFAST at 6 A. M. DINNER, at 12 M. Commence Work, after dinner, 12.45 P. M.

BELLS.

During January and December.

Morning Bells.	Dinner Bells.	Evening Bells.
First bell......5.00 A. M.	Ring out,..........12.30 P. M.	Ring out,..........7.00 P. M.
Second, "..........6.00..."	Ring in,..........1.05 P. M.	Except on Saturday Evenings.
Third,.."..........6.50..."		

From 1st of February to November 30th, inclusive.

Morning Bells.	Dinner Bells.	Evening Bells.
First bell,..........4.30 A. M.	Ring out,..........12.00 M.	Ring out at..........6.30 P. M.
Second, "..........5.30..."	Ring in,..........12.35 P. M.	Except on Saturday Evenings.
Third,.."..........6.20..."		

SATURDAY EVENING BELLS.

January,..........."RING OUT" each SATURDAY,..............at 4.00 P. M.		
February,..........." " "..............at 4.30..."		
March,..........." " "..............at 5.15..."		
April,..........." " "..............at 6.00..."		
May,..........." " "..............at 6.00..."		
June,..........." " "..............at 6.00..."		
July,..........." " "..............at 6.00..."		
August,..........." " "..............at 6.00..."		
September,..........." " "..............at 5.15..."		
October,..........." " "..............at 4.30..."		
November,..........." " "..............at 4.00..."		
December,..........." " "..............at 3.45..."		

YARD GATES will be opened at the first stroke of the bells for entering or leaving the Mills.

Speed Gates commence hoisting three minutes before commencing work.

Bells rang from morning until night.

10-hour workday for women and children.

What happened to these young women after they left Lowell's mills? Many returned to their homes and married. Others found new jobs just opening up for women. They traveled to Florida, Arkansas, and the Western states to help settle and build towns. Some became teachers, and a few started their own schools and libraries.

Lydia Hall studied law and became an acting U.S. treasurer. Margaret Foley went to Italy and became a famous sculptor. Harriet Farley and four other women became magazine editors. Harriet Hanson Robinson was one of 30 mill girls to publish books. Lucy Larcom became a college teacher and well-known poet. Sarah G. Bagley was a labor organizer and reformer and became the first female telegraph operator in the United States. She also opened a medical practice in New York.

Harriet Hanson Robinson

By the 1890s, young women from New England farms were going to college and had better job opportunities. Fewer came to work in the Lowell textile mills. In their place, immigrants from Ireland, Greece, Canada, Poland, Sweden, and other countries were hired. These men and women had come to the United States to get away from hunger and war in their countries. They found stability in the United States and jobs in the mills. But by the 1930s, the mills began to close, one by one. Other mills moved south, where land and labor were cheaper.

Today, many textile mill buildings remain in Massachusetts, but most no longer make cloth. Instead, they have been turned into housing, businesses, shops, and museums where visitors can go to learn about the life of the hard-working New England women. At one time, the mill girls were known as the "most superior class of factory worker

Immigrants, such as Portuguese women, replaced the New England workers.

ever to be found." Since then, they have been honored for improving women's rights and helping to set the standards for working conditions in American factories today.

The clock tower with its bells at the Boott Mill National Historic Site in Lowell

GLOSSARY

boardinghouse—a lodging house at which meals are provided

calico—cotton cloth that has small, brightly colored designs printed on it

domestics—household servants

immigrants—people who move from one country to live permanently in another

Industrial Revolution—a period from the middle 1700s to the middle 1800s of social and economic changes that took place during a transition from an agricultural and commercial society to an industrial society; the movement started in Great Britain and spread through Europe and the United States

Jew's harp—a small instrument held between the teeth and played with the fingers

lectures—talks given to an audience

mills—buildings where machines turn raw materials into finished products

textile—fabric made by weaving or knitting

DID YOU KNOW?

- When frontiersman Davy Crockett visited Lowell in 1834, he was given a wool suit made from cloth woven at a Lowell factory.

- U.S. presidents John Quincy Adams, Andrew Jackson, John Tyler, James Polk, and Abraham Lincoln visited the Lowell textile mills.

- Most of the mill girls owned only two dresses. The one she wore to work was covered with a large apron.

- Early New England textile mills relied on water for power. Because water was not dependable—too much in the spring, too little in the summer, and frozen in the winter—work was erratic. Mills often closed for a day or reduced production for months.

IMPORTANT DATES

Timeline

1813	In Waltham, Massachusetts, Francis Cabot Lowell opens his textile mill.
1817	Francis Cabot Lowell dies.
1822	Pawtucket Falls, on the Merrimack River in Massachusetts, is selected as a site for new textile mills.
1836	Women textile workers "turn out" to protest a rent increase in Lowell.
1840	*Lowell Offering* is the first magazine edited and published entirely by women.
1846	Sarah Bagley and the Lowell Female Labor Reform Association petition the Massachusetts Legislature for a 10-hour workday.
1847	Women textile workers pressure Lowell companies to add time to meal breaks, reducing the workday by 30 minutes.
1853	Textile workers throughout Massachusetts force textile companies to reduce the workday to 11 hours.
1874	The Massachusetts Legislature prohibits women and children from working more than 10 hours a day in a factory.

IMPORTANT PEOPLE

SARAH G. BAGLEY (1806–1883?)

Mill girl who organized and was the first president of the Lowell Female Labor Reform Association; in 1846, she became the first woman telegraph operator in the United States

HARRIET JANE FARLEY (1813–1907)

Author and co-editor of the Lowell Offering *from 1840 to 1845 and editor of the* New England Offering *from 1847 to the 1850s*

LUCY LARCOM (1824–1893)

Successful poet, author, teacher, and editor who wrote A New England Girlhood *about her experiences in the early Lowell textile mills*

FRANCIS CABOT LOWELL (1775–1817)

Son of a wealthy Massachusetts family who, with other investors, built and operated the first integrated cotton mill in the United States using machine designs he memorized during a visit to British textile mills

HARRIET HANSON ROBINSON (1825–1911)

Author and women's rights advocate who wrote Loom and Spindle *about her experiences working in the early Lowell textile mills; during the late 1800s, she fought for women's right to vote*

WANT TO KNOW MORE?

At the Library

Deitch, Joanne Weisman, ed. *The Lowell Mill Girls: Life in the Factory.* Carlisle, Mass.: Discovery Enterprises, 2002.

Denenberg, Barry. *So Far from Home: Diary of Mary Driscoll, an Irish Mill Girl, Lowell, Massachusetts, 1847.* New York: Scholastic, 1997.

McCully, Emily Arnold. *Bobbin Girl.* New York: Dial, 1996.

Patterson, Katherine. *Lyddie.* Thorndike, Md.: Thorndike Press, 1993.

Selden, Bernice. *The Mill Girls.* New York: Atheneum, 1983.

On the Web

For more information on the *Lowell Mill Girls*, use FactHound to track down Web sites related to this book.

1. Go to *www.facthound.com*

2. Type in a search word related to this book or this book ID: 075651262X

3. Click on the *Fetch It* button.

Your trusty FactHound will fetch the best Web sites for you!

On the Road

American Textile History Museum

491 Dutton St.

Lowell, MA 01854-4221

978/441-0400

To see a collection of machinery, tools, and workplace artifacts from the 18th century to the present

Lowell National Historical Park and Tsongas Industrial History Center

246 Market St.

Lowell, MA 01852

978/970-5000

To learn about the Industrial Revolution

Look for more We the People books about this era:

Angel Island

The Great Chicago Fire

Great Women of the Suffrage
    Movement

The Harlem Renaissance

The Haymarket Square Tragedy

The Hindenburg

Industrial America

The Johnstown Flood

Roosevelt's Rough Riders

A complete list of We the People titles is available on our Web site:
www.compasspointbooks.com

INDEX

About the Author

Alice K. Flanagan writes books for children and teachers. Since she was a young girl, she has enjoyed writing. She has written more than 70 books. Some of her books include biographies of U.S. presidents and their wives, biographies of people working in our neighborhoods, phonics books for beginning readers, and informational books about birds and Native Americans. Alice K. Flanagan lives in Chicago.